# EXPLORING GOD'S WORLD

## PICTURE AND BIBLE VERSES

# EXPLORING GOD'S WORLD

### PICTURE AND BIBLE VERSES

## JEAN ROBINSON

**ARPress**
ILLUMINATING IDEAS,
EMPOWERING VOICES

ARPress
45 Dan Road Suite 15
Canton MA 02021

Hotline:     1(888) 821-0229
Fax:         1(508) 545-7580

Ordering Information:
Quantity sales. Special discounts are available on quantity purchases by corporations, associations, and others. For details, contact the publisher at the address above.
Printed in the United States of America.

ISBN-13:    Paperback      979-8-89676-445-8
            eBook          979-8-89676-446-5
            Hardback       979-8-89676-456-4

Library of Congress Control Number: 2025915638

*The heavens declare the glory of God:*
*the skies proclaim the work of His hands.*

**Psalm 19:1**

*From the rising of the sun unto the going down of the same the Lord's name is to be praised.*

**Psalm 113:3**

*I will praise thee: for I am fearfully*
*and wonderfully made:*
*marvellous are thy works;*
*and that my soul knoweth right well.*

**Psalm 139:14**

*And God said, 'Let there be light,' and there was light.*

**Genesis 1:3**

*Make a joyful noise unto the Lord, all ye lands.*

**Psalm 100**

*O give thanks unto the Lord; for he is good: for his mercy endureth for ever.*

**Psalm 136:1**

*God is our refuge and strength, a very present help in trouble.*

**Psalm 46**

*For ye shall go out with joy and be led forth with peace:*
*the mountains and the hills shall break forth before you into*
*singing, and all the trees of the field shall clap their hands.*

**Isaiah 55:12**

*Trust in the Lord with all thine heart;
and lean not unto thine own understanding.*

**Proverbs 3:5–6**

*I will lift up mine eyes unto the hills,*
*from whence cometh my help.*
*My help cometh from the Lord,*
*which made heaven and earth.*

**Psalm 121:1–2**

*Be still and know that I am God:*
*I will be exalted among the heathen,*
*I will be exalted in the earth.*

**Psalm 46:10**

*O come, let us sing unto the Lord:*
*let us make a joyful noise*
*to the rock of our salvation.*

**Psalm 95**

*The Lord is my shepherd; I shall not want.*

**Psalm 23**

*It is a good thing to give thanks unto the Lord,*
*and to sing praises unto thy name, O most High*

**Psalm 92**

*Even there shall thy hand lead me,*
*and thy right hand shall hold me.*

**Psalm 139:10**

*Thy mercy, O Lord, is in the heavens:*
*and thy faithfulness reacheth unto the clouds.*
*Thy righteousness is like the great mountains:*
*thy judgments are a great deep:*
*O Lord, thou preservest man and beast.*

**Psalm 36: 5–6**

*The earth is the Lord's, and the fulness thereof; the world, and they that dwell therein.*

**Psalm 24**

*The Lord is slow to anger, and great in power,*
*and will not at all acquit the wicked:*
*the Lord hath his way in the whirlwind and in the storm,*
*and the clouds are the dust of his feet.*

**Nahum 1:3**

*And the peace of God, which passeth all understanding, shall keep your hearts and minds through Christ Jesus.*

**Philippians 4:7**

*For we walk by faith, not by sight:*

**2 Corinthians 5:7**

*Be strong and courageous.*
*Do not be afraid; do not be discouraged,*
*for the Lord your God will be with you*
*wherever you go.*

**Joshua 1:9**

*And Jesus said unto them, Because of your unbelief: for verily I say unto you, if ye have faith as a grain of mustard seed, ye shall say unto this mountain, remove hence to yonder place; and it shall remove; and nothing shall be impossible unto you.*

**Matthew 17:20**

*Pray without ceasing.*

**1 Thessalonians 5:17**

*The flowers appear on the earth:*
*the time of the singing of birds comes,*
*and the voice of the turtle is heard in our land.*

**Song of Solomon 2:12**

*This is the day the Lord has made:*
*let us rejoice and be glad in it.*

**Psalm 118:24**

# THE LORDS PRAYER
## Matthew 6: 9-13

"Our Father which art in heaven,
Hallowed be thy name.
Thy kingdom come.
Thy will be done
In earth, as it is in heaven.

Give us this day
Our daily bread.
And forgive us our debts,
As we forgive our debtors.
And lead us not into temptation,
But deliver us from evil:

For thine is the kingdom,
And the power,
And the glory,
For ever. Amen"

# THE BEATITUDES FROM THE
# SERMON ON THE MOUNT
### Matthew 5:3–12

"Blessed are the poor in spirit:
For theirs is the kingdom of heaven.

Blessed are they that mourn:
For they shall be comforted.

Blessed are the meek:
For they shall inherit the earth.

Blessed are they which do hunger and thirst after righteousness:
For they shall be filled.

Blessed are the merciful:
For they shall obtain mercy.

Blessed are the pure in heart:
For they shall see God.

Blessed are the peacemakers:
For they shall be called the children of God.

Blessed are they which are persecuted for righteousness' sake:
For theirs is the kingdom of heaven.

Blessed are ye, when men shall revile you, and persecute you, and
shall say all manner of evil against you falsely, for my sake.
Rejoice, and be exceeding glad: for great is your reward in heaven: for
So persecuted they the prophets which were before you.

*Let the floods clap their hands:*
*let the hills be joyful together*

**Psalm 98:8**

*I do set my bow in the cloud, and it shall be for a token of a covenant between me and the earth.*

**Genesis 9:13**

*There is a time for everything, and a season for every activity under the heavens.*

**Ecclesiastes 3:1**

*The hair on His head was white like wool, as white as snow, and His eyes were like blazing fire.*

**Revelation 1:14**

*He will be like a tree firmly planted by streams of water, which yields its fruit in its season and its leaf does not wither and in whatever he does, he prospers.*

**Psalm 1:3**

*Rejoice evermore.*

**1 Thessalonians 5:16**

*You will be blessed when you come in and blessed when you go out.*

**Deuteronomy 28:6**

*When I consider thy heavens, the work of thy fingers,
the moon and the stars, which thou hast ordained:
What is man, that thou art mindful of him?*

**Psalm 8:3–4**

*His lightnings enlightened the world:*
*the earth saw, and trembled.*

**Psalm 97:4**

*Jesus said unto him, If thou canst believe,
all things are possible to him that believeth.*

**Mark 9:23**

*Blessed is the pure in heart, for they will see God.*

**Matthew 5:8**

*See how the flowers of the field grow.*
*They do not labor or spin. Yet*
*I tell you that not even Solomon in*
*all his splendor was dressed like one of these.*

**Matthew 6:28–29**

*As for man, his days are as grass:*
*as a flower of the field, so he flourisheth.*
*For the wind passeth over it, and it is gone:*
*and the place thereof shall know it no more.*

**Psalm 103:15–16**

*In everything give thanks: for this is the will of God in Christ Jesus concerning you.*

**1 Thessalonians 5:18**

*Now the God of hope fill you with
all joy and peace in believing,
that ye may abound in hope,
through the power of the Holy Ghost.*

**Romans 15:13**

*O Lord our Lord, how excellent is thy name in all the earth! Who hast set thy glory above the heavens.*

**Psalm 8:1**

*And God said, Let the waters bring forth*
*abundantly the moving creature that hath life,*
*and fowl that may fly above the earth*
*in the open firmament of heaven.*

**Genesis 1:20**

*Behold the fowls of the air: for they sow not,*
*neither do they reap, nor gather into barns:*
*yet your heavenly Father feedeth them.*
*Are ye not much better than they?*

**Matthew 6:26**

*Ye are the light of the world.*
*A city that is set on an hill cannot be hid.*

**Matthew 5:14**

*And God created great whales,*
*and every living creature that moveth,*
*which the waters brought forth abundantly,*
*after their kind, and every winged fowl after his kind:*
*and God saw that it was good.*

**Genesis 1:21**

*The fowl of the air, and the fish of the sea,*
*and whatsoever passeth through the paths of the seas.*

**Psalm 8:8**

*Rest in the Lord, and wait patiently for him:*
*fret not thyself because of him*
*who prospereth in his way...*

**Psalm 37:7**

*And now abideth faith, hope, charity, these three;*
*but the greatest of these is charity.*

**1 Corinthians 13:13**

*And we have known and believed the love that God hath to us. God is love: and he that dwelleth in love dwelleth in God, and God in him.*

**1 John 4:16**

*Beloved, let us love one another: for love is of God: and every one that loveth is born of God, and knoweth God.*

**1 John 4:7**

www.ingramcontent.com/pod-product-compliance
Lightning Source LLC
Chambersburg PA
CBHW060333181225
36967CB00034B/294